MW01042189

THE SINFUL
SACRIFICE

A'JOHNNA WHITE

WRITERS REPUBLIC L.L.C.
515 Summit Ave. Unit R1
Union City, NJ 07087, USA

Website: *www.writersrepublic.com*
Hotline: *1-877-656-6838*
Email: *info@writersrepublic.com*

Ordering Information:
Quantity sales. Special discounts are available on quantity purchases by corporations, associations, and others. For details, contact the publisher at the address above.

Library of Congress Control Number:		2021921187
ISBN-13:	978-1-63728-948-8	[Paperback Edition]
	978-1-63728-949-5	[Digital Edition]

Rev. date: 12/01/2021

THE DARKNESS

Do you hurt too?
Does it feel like everyone is right but,
No one is true?
Do you feel numb but also every emotion all the time?
Can you express your emotions to yourself but,
When someone asks you say your fine?
See, I'm just like you and, you're just like me.
We express our feelings, so why can't they see?

Memories to forget
But won't be forgotten
Circling the drain
Yet I've already hit rock bottom

I can't escape these memories
Especially not these scars
I try to pray to Heaven
But all I see are stars
The words of what they say
Still haunt me everyday
And no matter how many miles I run
I can't escape the pain

A pain deeper than blood
A hurt bigger than my body
A depressed state of mind
That radiates more than the rays of the sun
I have created an energy that is darker
Than the night
And as empty as the bottle that lays
Shattered on the floor I stand on

A checker on the board
A hand on my side
A turn played too long
A bad memory left in my mind

Why is it that the person that's supposed to love me most
Is the cause of most of my pain and anger?
It makes me feel like I could get more love off the streets
From a stranger.
It's so strange that my mind cannot comprehend this
Situation I've been put in.
Pushed around.
Blinded.
Guided incorrectly.
This apple fell far from the tree and I refuse to let it
Infect me.
How can I say this without being "disrespectful"?
That you have been everything to me, except helpful.
You put me in the front row to a symphony put on by
You!
The drugs!
And the devil!
We're on two completely different levels because unlike you
With this life I try to be careful!
You have obviously settled for something
you know is wrong but you
Act like its right. It's actively and
dramatically draining your life!
And you continue to watch it happen
It the amount of my esteem that you continue to flatten
And this poorly beating heart that you keep on cracking.

Everything is too much
And nothing is enough
I am trying to be strong
But I think I'm too tough
I'm a master of complication so
It's never straight forward.

The deeper you cut
The pain will fade
It only takes one to drift away
My vision will blur
As I start to go numb
This is nothing,
There's more to come

Gambling with the devil almost took my life
"Put a piece of metal here and you'll be just fine".
Year after year I played his game
Yet it only brought my heart hate and shame,
Shame so high
No one could save me
Some nights were so bad the devil wouldn't even play me
He told me stop wasting his time
And do as he said
Some nights I prayed for a monster under my bed
Because somehow instead
That was better than
The demons in my head

Only judged by the world to be misunderstood
I'm done so wrong but I keep doing good
Tryin to state my points
But it's only black and white
No in-between the lines
So why put up a fight
We're tackled to the other side
Where there's a fence built high
No one can hear our pain
Or feel the tears we've cried
Cause we're just misunderstood
Drenched in an avalanche of lies
Where deception comes to memorize
In the middle of my restless
Poisoned nights
I am reminded of a word
That tells a story of a teen
MISUNDERSTOOD
And misunderstood is me

Time has passed and things have changed
New starts and beginnings have been made
I'm still processing so some things are the same
And the past is the past
So who's to blame?
Too much was told but even more was hidden
And if you connect the dots
Some of it is written
Written in the book of history
But in a humans eye it's still a mystery
A mystery that was opened and closed in a blink of
An eye
We all know they didn't even try
They didn't try to save a life
Or protect a heart
They took the entire book
And threw it in the dark

Manipulated by a love I thought was true
Why didn't they notice? No one had a clue!
Just in case no one told you, your pride really grew
Compared to you I was a baby, I was brand new
You took advantage and lied to my face
You stepped out of line and misused your place
I wrongfully trusted you and let you in my head
That doesn't mean I wanted you in my bed
My love was something you misread
I feel SO guilty but I didn't think it needed to be said
You were the "adult" and you manipulated me!
I didn't say anything because I didn't
know who they would believe
You were the monster under my bed
Only you weren't under it, but on top of it
And the thought of your presence truly makes me sick
I get sick to my stomach every time I hear your voice
And every time we were alone you
decided to make the bad choice
You made a choice that blinded my common sense
And ever since that night I don't feel so common
I tried not to let you damage take control
But this hurt is way past my thresh hold

All the lies you confessed to me
Just another notch in your
Twisted masterpiece

Left all alone in isolation with no reservation
Reflecting on the past with no hesitation
My mind is traveling at the speed of lightening
Yet the days are slow and exhausting
The wind is speeding down the street
And people are still crossing
No stop signs
No street lights
Just leaves falling like crazy

Lies and false accusations
Put into motion
Because of your reckless temptation
I have to recollect myself
Because it's causing aggravation

My pains and feelings are expressed on these walls
They come out when I'm all alone
When I'm around anyone else
I don't say anything at all
I am a vault with no combination
But the pattern in my head has no hesitation
The wheel keeps turning and there's no brake
I know what's happening
But I don't know what's at stake
I'm headed for my past
I want to turn around
I try to reach Jesus
But I keep falling down
So where's my motivation?
Where's my intuition?
It always my past
But with a new edition

The integrity to better myself still beats inside
I want to be free
But there's still too much to hide

Where is the hope that's
Supposed to come?

An iridescent soul plastered in grief
A magnified heart drenched in deceit

A girl that's lost
A girl that's broken and confused
Only to see that she is mangled and bruised
From the anger in her eyes
To the lies on her arms

So filled with anger and nowhere to put it
So use to doing things I know I shouldn't
But the fire within is breaking loose
So close to the heat
It's tearing the noose
The words burst out and I drop to the floor
There's flames everywhere
But no pain anymore

I am one who has yet to feel
I am one who has yet to heal
A timeline of resentment
And a face with no resistance
A river that only flows
But no sign of it shows
A drop in an ocean
Puts the poison in the potion
A twist in the wind
Makes it stop and start again

Only a dull shimmer in the sky of existence
A sunny day thrown in disguise is the difference
A world of hate
A world of peace
A hint of joy
And a pinch of grief
Where to end and where to start
But don't tell them too much
Because they'll tear you apart
Too much of this
And not enough of that
Soo much tranquility we're going on attack
You don't look like me
And I don't look like you
No one is ever right
Yet even being wrong is true

You can only skate for so long
And you're bound to fall down when
there's nowhere to hold on
So here
I'm asking you for help
I can only do so much by myself
You tell me to skate over there
And skate over here
But you always skate away when you start
To see my tears
I hate these wheels on my skates
I want to die
But I also want to see the pearly gates
I want to see them open up
But the more you ignore me
The more I want to jump

A trail of lies with no explanation
A girl that's lost and full of temptation

Just another statistic followed by a new therapist
A countless number of my peers wearing long sleeves
In the summer to cover their wrist
And a thousand lies is all that remains to exist
There are no more presents that lay in the presence of my soul
And I am left all alone to fill this everlasting hole
That has consumed my whole spirit
My spirit is still fighting but I can't feel it
I'm ashamed
I want my prayers to be enough but it's not
There are no more slots
For mistakes and feeling guilty
No one can save me from this self-induced penalty
I am trapped in my body and
Held captive in my own mind
Time is passing by and leaving me behind
I am not scared of the darkness and I think that's the problem
The statistics are rising and lies are evolving
There is no mystery not worth solving
So why didn't they notice!?

Do you care enough to look past my smile?
Because not even a mile down the road there I laid
Numb and afraid
Too scared to say a word or even
Open my eyes
This is not a disguise
Because even the stars in the sky don't shine the same
This is beyond the point of shame
Because so many times I've tried to reframe
And pick up the pieces
Piece after piece and I still can't sleep
Because the night keeps me awake with this feeling
I can't shake

Am I gay?
Am I straight?
Is it a choice?
Is it fate?
Where's the love?
I feel the hate!

I can't get over the fact of
How much you hurt me

I want help
But I don't know how to open up
I don't know what to say
Or who to say it to
I want to see the other side
But I don't know if I'll make it through

The burning pain has returned again
Reminding me of my past
As the day goes on my heart has stopped
Causing me to die
They're dressed in black
While my eyes are closed

Whew!
It was just a dream

This only confirms what I already knew
I should have never believed your promises because
You were the one who said you're through
I walked through hell multiple times for you
And you continued to leave
Part of me was relieved and another part couldn't breathe
You lied to my face and misused your authority
You broke every code in the book
Ethically and morally

Why chase someone who isn't even running
It is absolutely pointless
Eventually
You're only running for your own entertainment
Not to mention you completely forgot
where you're supposed to be going
So when you stop running your unaware of your surroundings
And have no clue at all which direction to turn back to
Because the whole time you thought you were
Enjoying the chase
In reality
You have only been running from the truth

Frustration and pain filing my body
Expanding the words pilling up in my mouth
With every step and every complaint
The more hostile tears appear to build up
I can't positively express the way I've been feeling
There is only one thing to do
One thing that I do best
My sighs become stronger
As my happiness continues to fade
There is only one thing left to do right in this moment

Oops, did I disappoint you again?

We wrote a story at the age of 16
We fell short and we ran out of ink
Our book closed and fell apart at the seams
It's nothing like fairytales and dreams
Now we're falling apart
It was never true from the start
We're crying tears from the sky
Thinking that our love would never die
But now it's gone
So here to another sad love poem

As the sun will set
And the stars will shine
I can't bear to play
So I press rewind.

A girl with no identity
A girl with a mask
A girl with a sore heart
A girl with no class
A girl that's dark and a girl that's imperfect
But when the pieces are put together she's a girl that's worth it
A girl that is loved no matter the weather
Even if her life isn't completely together
I'm a girl I'll love always and forever
I'm my own "person" even when i don't act clever
And God will be my shoulder to cry on whenever

At this point in my life I felt like I was running in circles and no one could help me but myself. I didn't exactly know how to help myself either. I got baptized on the 3rd of February, 2019. I wanted to make a change and fully surrendered myself to God. I soon came to find that being a follower of Christ is a lot harder than it seemed. I was trying to make all the right choices and repent from my sin but even then, I backslid and fell. I fell harder than ever. God convicted my heart a number of times, and as time went on I started to feel more and more like a burden. Not only to God but to all my friends and family. I have an outstanding support system but at this time I was nowhere near ready to accept their love and kindness. I was angry and bitter.

This next section is about really wanting that desire to seek God but also being brought down by the devil. I know God sees me. I know God hears me. Thank you friends and family, you've helped me more than you could see.

THE LIGHT

There is beauty in the pain
Flowers can't grow without the rain
And what once was a stain has been turned into a beautiful
Sunrise
You have to experience lows to appreciate the highs
Appreciate the sun that dances in the sky
The fuzzy feeling you get from looking into their eyes
Appreciate the sparks that fly from the stars
And the midnight wind from passing cars

In a house of lies
And a world of death
With a bleeding heart
Living in this house of distress
I just want to be happy
I just want to see the world
I don't want to be in this house
I don't want to be this girl
The world is a wonderful place but I'm stuck in the dark
And when I look in the sky
I can't see the stars
All I can see are the bruises on my heart
I don't want to be this way
I swear it's tearing me apart
I just want to be happy
I just want to see the world
I don't want to be in this house
I don't want to be this girl
I'm more than what you see
I'm stronger than you think
I'm not defined by these scars
I'm more than this broken heart
But now I'm happy
And the world is a beautiful place
I'm fixing up this house
With a smile on my face

As the world chills my skin
And the moonlight sparkles in my eyes
There is yet a tree buried right by my side
With marks from a thousand years
Which has been fertilized from those with a million tears
This is my home
So delicate to the touch
Yet I'm overwhelmed by its mesmerizing beauty
This is a night to remember
Sitting under the unknown sky
On the 5th of November

I think I'll be okay
I'm just going to continue to pray

How should I start this and what words should I say
Surprisingly I got out of bed today
I've been shown the slightest of hope
and now I'm all pumped up
But when I'm all alone I think that I've just lucked up
And the voices continue
Repeating that no one is coming to my rescue
But how can they help when they're
on the other side of the wall
Within my body I continue to stumble and I fall
I trip over my guilt and slip right into my past
I'm reminded of my pain so obviously
I relapse
And my lungs start to collapse as I hit the floor
I'm screaming to God
"I CANT DO IT ANYMORE"
I don't want to be here any longer please just
Take this pain
I guess you thought I was stronger
Please just end this game
Because I'm not in control and sometimes
I don't think you are either
Maybe it's the devil
Maybe he's grown higher
The devil threw me in the dark but you
have surrounded me with lights
Blessed me with people
But the devil still haunts me through the night

So I close my eyes and try to pray
Hoping I can join you in heaven one day
But the devil plays movies on the backs of my eyelids
Showing me my sins and all the times I've backslid
The devil shows me all the reasons I could never be loved
And the devil shows me why I shouldn't be trusted above
The devil reminds me of the times I've been abused and judged
But then something inside reminds me of your steadfast love
It consumes me and puts me in a state of peace
But then the devil shows up and promises lies to me
The devil says that it's fake
That it's too good to be true
He said no one is worthy
Not even you
So how do I do this
How do I listen
You reveal your love so why am I still resisting
Which way is right
Because I don't want to be left
I believe in you God I just want to be kept
I'm a captive of my mind
I have enslaved myself
And the devil keeps whispering "you don't need any help"
But I know that he's lying
I know it's not true
I know that all things were made and are done through you
So why do I listen to everything but the truth

Acceptance is key and I need to realize that it's okay to be me
It's okay to be optimistic
And to everyone who sees this
Just know that you're forgiven
Even for the things that you haven't yet committed
Your sins have been washed away and even to this day
Your life has been spoken over
Something so mighty, someone so worthy
Yes we go through tribulations but God
never leaves through the journey
God is with us always and forever
Just know you can call in him whenever
Because there's no one better
To reach out to when you're feeling the pressure
Or simply want to give him thanks
And to the ones that don't believe I just hope you can receive
This message in disguise
This is deeper than looking in the sky
Because within us there is a prize
It's called faith
And it's something you can't shake
And no matter how much I toss and turn
I continue to learn that God Almighty is higher than all
No matter how many time we fall

When I was struggling here's a question that I asked a lot.
If God really loved me why would he allow
me to go through so much pain?
Just why?

Only friends in a different universe
But put in this world so together we hurt
From our tears that form these rivers
To the awkward memories that still bring me shivers
There is only a dull shimmer in the sky of the earth
No face too bright
And no eyes too deep
But I have no belief that this grief will cease
Because my heart is weak and my eye will weep
And from week to week
I constantly watch you leave as you
Ignore these leaves that fall of my tree on
This November felt street
So here as I stand just know
That I can and I always will
I will push my way through because not even you
Will hold me down
I am not one person bound
Ive been lost but now I'm found
And I'm left to the sound of rivers that flow
So now you may go
Because I'm never alone and I have built a home
That beats in my chest
We were put to the test
But now we can rest so
Here's my goodbye as I wish you the best

Feel the light!
Without a star right here
Or sunshine over there
There is only fog clouding the air

As I write these words my mind finds things to say
As I face this world I start to find new ways
Ways that go against everything I know
I've started to realize I never felt at home
That's how I feel
It's like I'm stuck in a different world
And trapped from what's real
There's no music to my ears
Only being lured in by these tears
The same tears that you can't see
The kind of tears that scream
God why me!
This is the kind of pain I can't express to anyone but myself
It's the type of fear that stops me from asking for help
I'm in this by myself
Right?
I've don't so many 360's and I still don't see the light
But it's because I've been looking straight
And not up above
It's because I live by the flesh and not Gods love
It's because I think getting help is simply receiving a hug
Let that soak in and let me say it again
People can only do so much but
It's always God that wins

My family tried to help me
But they can't make me love Jesus
It's something Ive had to do on my own
Make that choice

Live for Him
Love Him

What kind of words will it take for you
To open your eyes
Why are you still driving when you've
Passed a million signs
I can only hold so much resentment
Before I let go
It feels like I can't move on until I let people know
You have hurt me in ways I can't explain
You have done things that have caused me more than pain
But I want you to know
That you are forgiven
By God and myself
And in order for this to work I need you
To get some help
This is in a poem because
I don't have the energy to shout
There is only one way to fix this
And I don't think you realize what is at risk

As the wind continues to move and the
sun continues to set and rise
My mind and body are stuck to believe my enemies lies
While my heart is set in the truth and with grace
The Lord says
"Stay down and I will look to your enemies face.
You are my perfectly imperfect child
And even after all you mistakes I will
still choose you from the crowd.
Remember that I will always leave the 99 to chase after you
No matter the thickness of the clouds.
I will still see you
You are not forsaken but loved whole heartedly
Even when you run
You're still a part of me".

Thank you for that Jesus

I was an unclean soul with an ongoing battle in my mind
My soul was losing and didn't care what was left behind
I was nowhere to be found yet somehow
I was watching my life go by
Someone or something was in control of me
I knew it wasn't right but I still chose not to see
I didn't want to face the music and
See the pain that I had caused
I didn't want to think about being strapped to that
bed and screaming until my throat was raw
I didn't want to think about the awful
things I yelled at that guy
I didn't believe that all I had to do was
Try
Try to have faith or hope for better days
Try to have peace
And rejoice through the grief
I didn't know that a flip of a switch could open my
Heart
Soul
And eyes
And then is when I realized
That when the switch was off
I was believing the devils lies

It's a feeling unknown yet such a heavenly gift
A gift from you to me
Shining through the morning sunlight mist
I sing in your name
And pray for your plans
How could it be
You're such a kind and loving Man
Yes
I seek for you deeply
And you continue to keep me
So what will come of this day
I pray it is of your will
And that this feeling will stay

I hope this finds you at the right time
I hope you know
If you're with God you'll be just fine
Embrace being a child of God
Find yourself in Jesus
Because
He's the only one that truly sees us

DEDICATED TO THE 400 FAM

Here's to a love I found in a facility
Here's to a love that's thicker than blood
Here's to a love that's helped me find myself
Here's to a love that helped me organize the books on the shelf
You've shown me light in the darkness
And beauty in the pain
You've helped me face the music and
Embrace the rain
You've sat with me and listen to my river stream by
I just pray that you keep your head held high
In this facility
From the
Pain
Anger
And hurt
That I've seen
I just hope this means
I'll never see you again
At least not in here
I hope the next time you shed a tear
That you can remember feel and hear
The love coming from inside of me
Know that you are a perfectly imperfect
Masterpiece
That no matter the weather or the fear of the storm
It's always inevitable that the rainbow will form
I'm truly torn that I can't take the hurt from your body

And replace it with healing
So I'll end it with this
Know your worth and believe it in your heart
That you deserve the best
Find genuine peace and let you
Heart
Body
Soul
And mind
Humbly rest
Even as beautiful as snow can be
It still holds danger
Sometimes eyes are deceiving and it just builds the anger
So be someone's safe haven
Be someone's release
We are resilient
So let's cease the grief!

~AJ

CPSIA information can be obtained
at www.ICGtesting.com
Printed in the USA
BVHW031638180222
629427BV00002B/75